WALKER BOOKS
AND SUBSIDIARIES
LONDON • BOSTON • SYDNEY • AUCKLAND

On a **coral reef** in the big blue sea,
count the ocean creatures

1, 2, 3.

Coral is alive.
It is made up
of thousands
of tiny animals.

When lots of corals
grow close together,
it is called a reef.

Many amazing creatures
make their homes on a
coral reef.

1

One giant whale shark.

Whale sharks are the largest
fish in the sea but they eat the
smallest of plants and animals.

Some whale sharks can grow as long as a bus!

2 **Two** shy dugongs.

Dugongs love to graze on seagrass.
That's why some people call them sea cows.

3 **Three** playful clownfish.

Clownfish live in among the wavy tentacles of the stinging sea anemone.

They have a slimy coat that protects them from getting stung.

4 **Four** clever dolphins.

Dolphins can blow rings of air bubbles.

They are one of the smartest animals on the planet.

5 **Five** stripy sea snakes.

Sea snakes use a flat paddle-shaped tail to help them swim.

Even though sea snakes live under the water, sooner or later they need to come up for air.

 **Six** hungry turtles.

Green turtles always eat their vegetables – seaweed and sea lettuce.

They are one of the world's largest sea turtles.

7 **Seven** busy parrotfish.

Parrotfish have around 1000 teeth that they use to crunch up coral. Later, they poop out the chomped-up coral as sand.

8 Eight spotted rays.

When rays swim, they look like
birds flapping their wings.

Eagle rays have poisonous
spines on their long, thin tails.

 **Nine** wobbly jellyfish.

Jellyfish are not fish.
They are sea creatures mostly made up of water.

Moon jellyfish look a lot like floating moons.

 **Ten** blue starfish.

Starfish use their hundreds of
tiny tube-like feet to move around.

When a starfish loses an arm,
it can grow a new one.
That's handy!

11

Eleven snappy crabs.

Crabs have ten legs. The front two are called claws and are used to grab things. The other eight are used for walking.

12 **Twelve** tired seahorses.

Seahorses wrap their tails around sponges, coral or sea plants to stop from floating away.

Seahorses will never win a race. They are one of the slowest fish in the ocean.

All on a **coral reef**
in the big blue sea.

Coral reefs are important because
they keep the sea healthy.

A healthy reef means a healthy sea.
A healthy sea means a healthy planet.

For Zimi, Easton, Banjo and Ethan - FL

This edition published 2022 by Walker Books Ltd
87 Vauxhall Walk, London SE11 5HJ

2 4 6 8 10 9 7 5 3 1

© 2020 Frané Lessac

The right of Frané Lessac to be identified as author and illustrator
of this work has been asserted by her in accordance with the
Copyright, Designs and Patents Act 1988

This book has been typeset in Jennerik, Klepto, Printer and Paytone One

Printed in China

ISBN 978-1-4063-9852-6

www.walker.co.uk

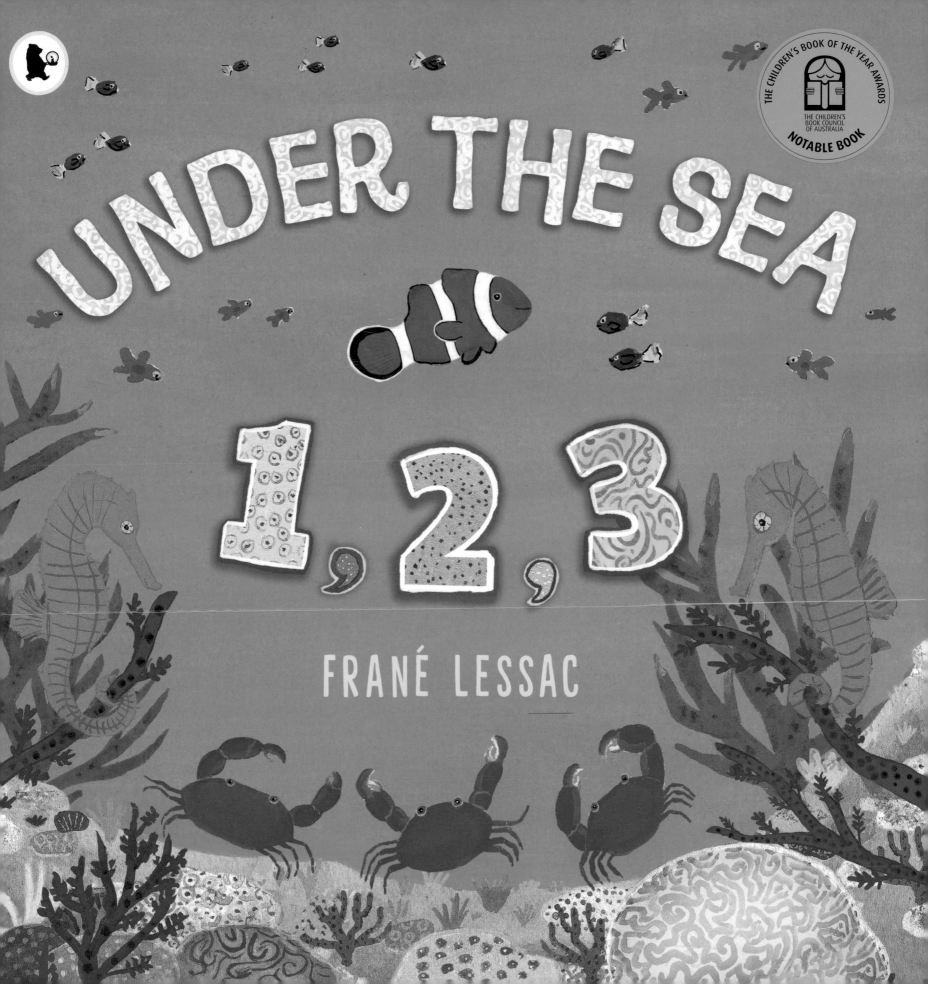

UNDER THE SEA

1, 2, 3

FRANÉ LESSAC